The Royal Garden of Pefkou

Or, in Medieval French
Le Jardin Regal du Pin

A Study of Fruit Consumption
in Medieval Nicosia

William Woys Weaver

MOUFFLON PUBLICATIONS

MOUFFLON PUBLICATIONS LTD.
20 Costi Palama
Aspelia Buildings
Apartment E1
1096 Lefkosia, Cyprus

www.moufflonpublications.com
publishing@moufflon.com.cy

Copyright © William Woys Weaver 2006

All rights reserved.
No part of this book may be reproduced or transmitted in any form
by any means, electronic, mechanical, photocopying, recording, or
otherwise, without the prior written permission of the publisher.

ISBN 9963-642-25-x

Design and typesetting by Toby Macklin

Printed and bound in Cyprus by Imprinta Ltd.

Preface

This study of the medieval garden at Pefkou provides a unique glimpse into life in Cyprus during the Lusignan period (1192–1489). It has been written as much for Cypriots curious about their culinary past as for readers unfamiliar with Cyprus and its complex history. For this reason, I have taken extra pains to explain terms and concepts so that this monograph can stand on its own as an example of a holistic approach to garden, food, and diet. This is a philosophical approach that I have taken in all the books I have written to date, and I hope that as a result my readers will see medieval Cyprus in a new light.

My interest in the gardens and horticultural heritage of Cyprus began ten years ago when I came to the island for a conference on ethnological food research. At the time, I was collaborating with the late Maria Dembinska of Poland on bringing out an American edition of her seminal study of food consumption in medieval Poland. We intersected in Cyprus for the conference, but so did our work on the book because King Peter I of Cyprus visited Cracow in 1365, and King John II of Cyprus was to have married Polish princess Jadwiga Jagiello in 1432. She died before the mission to Poland was able to bring about the wedding, but the large entourages of people moving back and forth now pose many, many questions about direct contacts between Europe and the Eastern Mediterranean.

It became immediately clear to me that the connection with Cyprus had not been well researched. The more I delved into the subject, the more I realized that Cyprus was a key conduit to the West for foods, wines, and other aspects of medieval lifestyle, even falconry. This encouraged me to dig deep into what was known about Cyprus during the period of the Lusignan monarchy. As a food and plant historian, I could not have chosen a more fascinating subject. My interest in Pefkou evolved out of an ongoing effort to catalogue what is known about the food plants of medieval Cyprus. Nothing remains of Pefkou today. Even the site has been destroyed, so what little we know about it comes to us from the document analyzed in the pages that follow.

A push from my energetic Cypriot colleague Maria Evangelou to initiate the restoration of a medieval garden at St Nicholas of the Cats, together with an invitation from Moufflon Publications to publish this monograph, have now launched into print the results of some of my research. I am deeply grateful to

Maria, to Helen Pavlou who was an immense help with Cypriot dialect terminologies, to Byzantine specialist Andrew Dalby for useful advice, and to all the other individuals – among them Adrienne Hall and Dr Costas Gregoriou of the Cyprus Department of Agriculture – who helped me construct the story of this most unusual garden record. Finally, warm thanks must be given to Dr Yvonne LeBlanc of the Hill School near Philadelphia, who polished the medieval French records into elegant English. Her knowledge of medieval French made her highly suitable for this task.

William Woys Weaver,
Professor of Food Studies
Drexel University
Philadelphia USA

The Garden of Pefkou

When Count Gabriel Capodilista of Padua visited the fief of Episkopi along the south coast of Cyprus in 1458, he was astonished by the high state of cultivation, by the extensive sugar cane fields, and especially by the magnificent private gardens belonging to Andrea Cornaro of Venice. He 'stayed a little while in this village and saw some of the most lovely gardens of oranges, citrons and carobs, and another sort of tree called *musa* [banana], which produces fruit very much like small cucumbers; when they are ripe they are yellow and very sweet to savour … these gardens and fields are watered by irrigation ditches, and *colocasia* [taro] and squills grow there in abundance.'[1]

Even in Cyprus, where exquisite fruits were easy to grow and commonplace on the tables of the aristocracy, medieval records are clear in differentiating fruits of the rich from fruits enjoyed by the villagers and the urban poor. With the exception of grapes, pomegranates, and figs – which were universal in medieval Cypriot diet – fruits consumed by the poor were mostly melons or watermelons (which they could grow on their small plots) or fruit gathered from the wild. Much of the orchard fruit belonged to the Cypriot nobility, to the Latin Church and its many orders, or to Greek monasteries. The diet of the native Greek monks was vegetarian, so fruit played an important role in their way of life. The monastery was in fact one certain way to escape the poverty of the feudal village.

For the nobility who aped the *haute cuisine* of the royal court, it was not considered healthy to eat most fruits raw. Vegetables were always cooked, although villagers did eat raw onions, much to the disdain of the Frankish nobility. Fruit was usually processed in some way to temper its humoural characteristics: hot, cold, moist, dry according to the tenets of Galenic dietary rules. Or, as in the case of the juice of sour pomegranates and oranges, fruit played a key role as a component in tempering the qualities of other foods.[2] Regardless, during the golden age of the Lusignan kingdom (1192–1374), the lavish eating habits of the upper classes in Cyprus provided a model for the rest of Europe. Cypriot was actually a term for a recognizable international style of cookery during the late Middle Ages. Broadly speaking, it survives in the body of recipes scattered in medieval manuscripts under the generic heading of *vyaunds de Chypre*. But the perceptions of Europe were one thing; how Cypriots ate on the local level was quite another matter.

One of the most useful documents relating to this highly stratified system of food consumption is a 1468 agreement of transfer dealing with a royal garden in Nicosia called *du Pin* in French or in Greek *Pefkou* (The Pine) in reference to a large and probably ancient pine tree that was its defining feature. The document concerns the renouncement of rights and quit-rents of an Armenian-Cypriot, George of Sis, who transferred tenant obligations to a wealthy Arab Christian called Theodore, son of Saïd the Syrian. These Syrians lived at Laxia, a feudal village to the south of Nicosia. The land belonging to Pefkou abutted property owned by the parish church of St Eustace and by the monastery of St Nicholas of Quillac. A translation of the agreement is provided at the end of this study (p. 37).

The text was preserved in a collection of legal records known as *Le livre des remembrances de la secrète du royaume de Chypre*. This unique collection of documents deals with the proceedings of the royal treasury and dates from the years 1468–9, during the reign of James II, nicknamed 'Apostle'. The text was edited and published in the original French in 1983.[3] This is one of a handful of books that are known to have survived from the once extensive royal library, which disappeared when the Turks looted Nicosia in 1570. The original manuscript is now in the collection of the Vatican Library.

James II was the son of King John II (1414–58) by his Greek mistress Maria of Patras. Although he was illegitimate, his doting father made him archbishop of Nicosia, an appointment never recognized by the Pope. After the death of King John II, James was driven out of the kingdom by his half-sister, Queen Charlotte de Lusignan. With the help of the sultan of Egypt, James II returned with an army, overthrew Charlotte, and freed Famagusta (Ammochostos) from Genoese occupation. He then proclaimed himself king.

To legitimize his position against the Genoese, James married Caterina Cornaro of Venice. While hunting in 1473, he was allegedly poisoned by the Cornaros, who eventually forced Caterina to abdicate the throne in 1489, thus bringing the *haute court* to an end and opening an era of total Venetian domination of the island. This tumultuous period in Cypriot history is described in detail in the chronicle of George Boustronios, which serves as a useful time frame for *Le livre des remembrances*.[4] Some of the documents recorded in *Le livre* reflect an attempt by James II to settle political scores through expropriation of property or by revising old contracts so that they would be more favourable to the Crown. Others deal with day-to-day household matters.

Regarding the tenant of Pefkou, it is hard to say why George of Sis gave up his occupancy of such a valuable garden, but give it up he did. References to a columned doorway with a missing plinth or base, to a large section of missing hedge, and to various abandoned relics connected to the irrigation system may imply that he was not able to keep up the terms of his occupancy due to a shortage of cash or some other personal circumstance. The Egyptian forces that swept James II into power also did a considerable amount of looting, especially when it came to property belonging to James's enemies. It is possible that Sis was pressured out because of family loyalties to Charlotte de Lusignan, who had already left the island by that time.

His name does not appear among the 1467 list of nobles who accompanied Charlotte into exile, although there is an individual called Antoinus de Si who might be a relative.[5] Given the possibility of inconsistent spelling in this list, it is conceivable that this person's name was Sis; perhaps father or brother, we do not know. If this is the case, however, then the stars of the Sis clan had definitely fallen; in the violent politics of medieval Cyprus, the perceived guilt of one family member could easily affect the safety of the rest. It was because the ground rents and all feudal rights to the garden belonged to the king that there was a need for the royal treasury to intervene and, for income purposes, to order an inventory of the improvements on royal land. The much impoverished James II was a great believer in strange but effective taxes; as a half-Greek with a winning personality and very good looks, he could cite royal precedent at every legal turn.

The Lusignans often resorted to taxing extensive gardens of the sort found at Episkopi and Pefkou when they needed to raise money for the royal treasury. This was one of several ways that the Crown could dip into the cash reserves (mostly hidden) of the nobility, wealthy merchants, and in the case of Pefkou and its quit-rents, even the petty gentry. Furthermore, for the purposes of taxation and inheritance in medieval Cyprus, it was possible to own trees or grapevines on someone else's land. Thus the plants enumerated in the Pefkou document were legally speaking separate from the ground in which they grew. This tax structure was carried over from Byzantine practice and surfaces in many other documents from the period. It is this plant list that makes the Pefkou inventory so valuable.

Pefkou and its Location in Medieval Nicosia

Pefkou is described in French as a *jardin*, a term generally used in Cyprus for large, open plantings arranged orchard-fashion, but containing high-value plants as opposed to vegetables. Vegetables could be interplanted among the trees, but they were not the primary focus of a *jardin*. Another word for a garden was *courtille*, specifically an enclosed garden, the sort one might find beyond the courtyard of an urban palace. It was here that Cypriot nobles kept pet monkeys, caged birds, and peacocks. The intimate enclosed gardens at the Alhambra in Spain had their counterparts in medieval Cyprus and they were always called *courtilles*. Based on these terminological distinctions, we can presume that Pefkou was not an ornamental pleasure garden, but rather a fancy orchard in which the trees and shrubs may have been arranged in a visually pleasing manner.

The actual property was located to the south or southwest of Nicosia in an area of the city once contained within the original Byzantine walls. This part of the city, now covered with modern buildings, was cleared in 1567 when the Venetians demolished large parts of Nicosia in order to build the present fortifications. Doubtless the rubble of many architectural treasures is buried within those ramparts. The precise location of the garden property is not known, but one useful landmark is the neighbouring tract belonging to St Nicholas of Quillac (Kellaki), a satellite monastery of St Nicholas of Quillac once situated in the village of Kellaki near Limassol, and part of a chain of monasteries governed by St Nicholas of the Cats on Cape Gata. Like the garden, St Nicholas of Quillac was destroyed in 1567, and there are no visible monastic ruins present today at Kellaki village. The name of the place means 'the cells' (from the Greek word *kelli*), as in the type of cell or hut inhabited by monks. Quillac, as the village was known in French, belonged to the Order of St John of Jerusalem and was the headquarters of their best wine-producing estates. It is mentioned often in the records of this order. Since St Nicholas of the Cats was a royal monastery (a monastery subject to the Latin Patriarch of Jerusalem and supported by the Crown), it would follow that the properties connected to it also fell under royal protection.

It appears that Pefkou was some type of royal *presterie* let out to rent. In the manor system of medieval Cyprus, a *presterie* was a hamlet or piece of land attached to a larger estate (*casale*) but not adjacent to it. This class of patchwork land ownership was largely rural, but since the term shows up in other urban land transfers, it appears to have applied as well to property within the city walls.[6] Legally speaking, Pefkou was a *presterie* attached to the royal palace, at that time a fourteenth-century building that stood opposite the Cathedral of Holy Wisdom (the palace was demolished by the British in the early twentieth century). In short, the tenants of Pefkou rented land that was a legal extension of the king's own residence, a cozy arrangement for those in royal favour, yet a perilous and impermanent situation subject to shifting political fortunes.

Unlike the crowded medieval cities of Europe, Nicosia was spread out over a large area with extensive gardens and even farmland interspersed among houses and palaces. Furthermore, it is clear in many early documents that the Lusignans at one time owned considerable acreage within the city walls for the purpose of producing food for the court. Later, as they built more and more palaces in the countryside, food production shifted to the royal *allodia* (lands personally owned by the monarch). This shift opened up opportunities for selling or leasing urban property that was no longer critical to the royal household.

According to the inventory, the property called Pefkou consisted of an irrigated fruit garden enclosed by a hedge, unirrigated fields, and three spacious houses all with their own entrance gates leading into courtyards behind. These houses were characterized as *ostels* (*hôtels*) meaning that they were considered substantial, on the scale of a large townhouse or mansion. With 18 rafters (one of the Cypriot measures for taxing dwellings), the buildings were definitely long, but not overly large by Nicosia standards. By contrast, a peasant's cottage in this period might have no more than four or five rafters holding up a flat, clay-covered roof or a roof covered with reed mats and thatch.

In all likelihood, the buildings at Pefkou were squat (built low to protect them from earthquake damage), constructed of cut stone, roofed with tiles, and two stories in height, since the ground-level floor in houses of this type was used for storage and livestock. Due to the vagueness of the document it is difficult to speculate about the functions these buildings served; one may simply have been a gatehouse. However, most structures owned by the Crown were of better construction than the common mud-brick houses found in and around Nicosia at this time. The Lusignans even imported foreign craftsmen to create buildings that imitated similar structures in France. The picture that emerges from the data is of a small, affluent working farm with a church and monastery right beside it. This was precisely the type of urban real estate that the rulers of Cyprus either kept for themselves as income producing lands, rented out to favourites, or gave away as gifts (usually life tenures) to individuals whose loyalty and service made them candidates for such rewards.

It was through this system of rewards that individuals were able to raise themselves up above the level of commoners, and it is no coincidence that nearly all of the parties mentioned in the garden contract are gentry or nobles of one kind or another – property owners who derived their livelihood from sources other than manual labour. In Cyprus this mélange of native Greeks and foreigners formed the backbone of the royal bureaucracy and is well evidenced by the range of nationalities represented in the Pefkou contract. Several of the individuals are addressed in French as *sire*, a clear sign of their class distinction.

Nearly all of the men involved in facilitating the transaction were royal bureaucrats whose presence was required for the execution of the document. This took place at a burgess court overseen by Jayme Zaplana, viscount of Nicosia. A royal tax man was present to record the transaction in French. Most of the men had two names, which set them apart from peasants and the lower nobility. Much is known about Viscount Jayme Zaplana, a Catalan whose involvement in the murder in 1473 of Andrea Cornaro (the uncle of Queen Caterina) ended in the loss of his houses in Nicosia, and the seizure of his velvet clothes, his falcons and his feudal villages, all of which is documented in the chronicle of George Boustronios. Philip Ciba was the bailiff or chief magistrate of the royal treasury and as such was empowered to enforce the will of the king. Sir Thomas Petropoulo was a noble of Greek Cypriot stock and one of the treasury officials.

The other officials were Andrea Bibi and Sir Peter Goul, both Christians of Syrian descent. The Goul family was extremely powerful; its feudal manor, centred on the modern village of Choulou, north of Paphos, was once the seat of extensive rural holdings, until it passed into the hands of the Montolif clan. The name Bibi derives from the Arabic name *habib* or *habibi* and, like Goul, is an indication of an Arab rather than Cypriot origin.

Sir Simon Stranbailli came from an old line of royal office holders long connected with the Lusignan court. Sometimes his name is written Strambali, as though it were Italian, but there is no doubt that he was a Frankish Cypriot. Another Cypriot was Father Sava Prokopis, in all likelihood the priest at Saint 'Efthihi' nearby – this is properly written in Greek as Ayios Evstathios, in English as Saint Eustace. As the parish priest living next door, he could make a fair judgment of the garden's contents and probably knew it well. Because he could read and write (and seems to have known a certain amount of Latin), he was appointed by Zaplana to oversee the appraisal and render up a document listing the inventory of plants and structures. Furthermore, as a man of the cloth, it was his place to guarantee that there was no deception on the part of the appraisers and head gardener, whose name, oddly enough, is not mentioned in the document. He is simply referred to by his Greek title, *protoquiporo* (πρωτοχηπουρός). We can safely assume that he worked for a salary and was a free citizen of Nicosia, otherwise he would not have been permitted to help with the inventory. The garden crews under his direction were probably serfs attached to the estate.

In addition to Latin, most of the better educated class of nobles in Cyprus spoke French, as well as Greek or Arabic with varied proficiency, so the conversation the treasury men had on the day they executed the transfer probably weaved in and out of all four languages. In any event, they would have had to address the head gardener (if he were present) and probably also the priest in Cypriot Greek. This highlights a fascinating picture of the cosmopolitan nature of medieval Nicosia and the kind of ethnic mix that existed amongst its population. While none of the players named in the contract would have doubted for a moment the supremacy of the Crown and the French-speaking court, it is easy to detect the influence of Armenians, Syrians, and Greeks on the Frankish culture of the Lusignans. Most of the fruit trees in the inventory bear French names derived from Cypriot Greek words; many garden terms came from the Arabic spoken by Arab Christians.

The Maronites and other Arab Christians living on the island were conduits for cultural exchanges with the Muslim mainland. Indeed, the *ttavas*, the universal earthenware bake-pot in the lowland areas of Cyprus, is a form of medieval Syrian origin.[7] Perhaps more pertinent to this essay, the Syrian Christians were also sophisticated gardeners and produce vendors; many were cooks, confectioners or pastry chefs, and they formed a large and affluent artisan class in many Cypriot towns. They were also protected by the Crown and allowed to hold their own burgess courts.

Of course, the central figure in the document is George of Sis. His name is written many ways in Cypriot records, often in French as Sasi/Sasin or Sisy, or in Greek as Sisou, the Cypriot 'ou' taking the place of the 'y'. There are individuals in Cyprus today who bear the name Sisou. It means simply that they originated from the city of Sis, the ancient capital of the Armenian kingdom of Cilicia (presently in southeast Turkey). The family name is probably derived from an abbreviated administrative title, such as castellan of Sis or bailiff of Sis, some official function that ceased upon their migration to Cyprus.

The kingdom of Cilicia recognized the Pope as its spiritual leader and was at one time aligned with Cyprus through intermarriage with the Lusignans. The kingdom fell to the Seljuk Turks in 1375 and was gradually ethnically cleansed of all its non-Muslim inhabitants. The last of the Greeks and Armenians were purged in the 1920s.[8] It is important to keep in mind that the kings of Cyprus inherited the crown of Armenia in 1393, so émigré Armenian nobles living in Cyprus were feudally bound to the Lusignans. Under that constraint they could count on employment at the royal court according to their rank and political savvy, and this seems to have been the case with the Sis family.

For many centuries Cyprus served as a place of refuge for Armenians displaced by Muslim incursions into their ancient homeland. But several Byzantine emperors also moved Armenians to the island, both to repopulate villages decimated by disease and natural disasters and to exile troublemakers among the Armenian nobility. It is known that Emperor John Kaloyannis captured the fortress town of T'il Hamdun (modern Turkish Toprakkale) in Cilicia and as punishment for the insurrection in 1136–7 moved the entire population to Cyprus. Thus there was already a large indigenous Armenian community on the island when the Lusignan kingdom was established in 1192. Of the three Armenian quarters in medieval Nicosia the largest was in the vicinity of the present Paphos Gate. There was also an Armenian quarter in Famagusta. The fact that George of Sis was renting the garden of Pefkou should not necessarily imply that he also lived on the premises. He was required to maintain it in good order, but could have owned a primary residence somewhere else in the city. He was probably a descendant (grandson?) of Peter of Sis who served as *maître de l'hôtel de la reine* (steward or chief butler) to Queen Charlotte de Bourbon, the second wife of King Janus. Another branch of the Sis family migrated to Poland shortly after 1375. They were joined to the Polish noble clan of Jastrzebiec and began writing the family name as Sasin.

The one other person whose name stands out in the transfer is Lady Marie Fougère, who is definitely a person of noble rank. Her name is repeated several times in the document. Only a woman of high social status would have been able to represent herself in a legal transaction. Normally in this period, such business was handled by a trusted male relative or her husband. In the case of Pefkou, it would appear that she had at some point given over her rights directly to George of Sis. The date of that transaction is not mentioned in the original document. It is a very real possibility that the Fougère-Sis arrangement had been confirmed by Queen Charlotte or her father, but was now being revisited by King James II, who was essentially replacing Sis with one of his own political cronies. It would not be surprising if it turned out that the king owed Saïd the Syrian a large sum of money. This may be reading too much into the document, yet there is a political 'odour' about the transaction because of who the Fougères were and their connection with the House of Savoy, the hated enemies of James II.

We do not know much about Marie Fougère, but in 1443 a 'dame de Frugière' [sic] accompanied Princess Agnes de Lusignan to Savoy, when the princess married Louis, later Duke of Savoy.[9] The princess was half-aunt to King James II and the mother of Queen Charlotte's husband, Louis of Savoy (son of the duke and Queen Charlotte's own first cousin). While not part of the high ruling nobility – the king's twelve barons as they were styled – this would suggest that the Fougères were members of a second tier of inner court circles, and that the woman who went to Savoy with the princess was probably a lady in waiting. If she were the same as the former tenant of Pefkou, this would have made her an absentee land owner in Cyprus, an extremely common situation in this period. Regardless, the fact that the garden was once occupied by a Fougère suggests that this was a neighbourhood of choice real estate. It further confirms the hypothesis that much of the land in the area belonged to the Lusignans at one time or another, and this means that George of Sis was himself a person of some note, or he would not have gained tenancy with royal approval. In short, the garden at Pefkou represents a type of urban property occupied by petty nobles employed by the Crown.

The Plants at Pefkou

I have rearranged the original inventory in order to list the plants alphabetically in English. Following the English name, I have provided the scientific nomenclature based on Lyle's *Fruit & Nuts* (Portland, 2006), and to a lesser extent on R. D. Meikle's *Flora of Cyprus* (London, 1977). I then provide the original Cypriot Frankish term and the Cypriot Greek from which it is derived.[10] I have tried to avoid speculating on the origins of many of the Cypriot terms because in several cases this is still an area of controversy. I do try to offer some comments on each fruit based on what is known about it in Cyprus during the 1400s. One pair of trees, which I have listed tentatively under sorb apple, is still pretty much a question mark because the name applied to it in French is not a known term in Cypriot Frankish.

It is also surprising that no almonds, bananas, hazelnuts, lemons, pears, pistachios, or quince are mentioned, because they were definitely known of in Cyprus at the time and many were subject to royal taxes in the assizes of 1250.[11] On the other hand, a good number of these items were luxury foods and were only mentioned in connection with gardens and orchards belonging to the high nobility or to very rich merchants. The Cornaros are an excellent example of this type of owner, for while they did not possess a hereditary title, they were powerful merchant-aristocrats both in Venice and in Cyprus. Their primary source of wealth was derived from sugar plantations.

If the humid coastal gardens of Episkopi represent the orchard gardens of royalty and wealth, then the walled gardens of Pefkou represent an old-fashioned type of orchard garden, at least in its selection of plants, a garden that was in many ways more like the Byzantine gardens on the island than the more diverse Renaissance pleasure gardens planted later by the Venetians. We must also keep in mind that Pefkou was a work in progress – some trees were old, others were recently planted – so there is no reason to eliminate the possibility that dates, pears, quinces, lemons or anything else may eventually have found a place on the grounds. There was certainly room for expansion, and the climate around Nicosia is still ideal for all of these plants.

Although Queen Catarina Cornaro maintained a summer palace at Potamia in the breezy hill country between Nicosia and Famagusta, the main pleasure garden for the Lusignans was located at Château de la Cave about four miles southeast of Athalassa. The palace, which took its name from an immense wine cellar on the site, was constructed in the 1370s on a high mesa by King Peter II and further improved by King James I in 1385. The flat top of the hill was carved out to make room for a huge pond-like cistern that supplied water to the surrounding gardens below and also served as a fish pond, especially for eels. The waterworks employed for moving the water up or down the hill was referred to by the Franks as a *berquil*, a term borrowed from Arabic *birket* and used in reference to Persian waterwheels associated with ponds or cisterns. In fact the term, as loosely used by the Franks, seems to cover the whole irrigation system fed by the waterwheels, not just the cistern, although a cistern was inevitably part of it. This technology was not known in France at the time, hence the need to expropriate an Arabic word for it.

Persian waterwheels were introduced into Egypt and Cyprus, and as far west as Spain, during the reform of Byzantine agriculture in the sixth century AD. After the Arab conquest of North Africa, they became a symbol of Arab agriculture. They were constructed in the form of large wooden wheels, often several working simultaneously, to which earthenware jars were attached; the jars went down mouth-end first into a well or cistern and came up the other side full of water. The water was then emptied into a system of low walls with channels cut in the top or even into small aqueducts and pipes which conveyed it throughout the garden. The wheels were turned by donkeys or camels; in Mesaoria (the central valley of Cyprus) windmills often supplied the power.

We know that there was a device like this at Pefkou because of the inclusion in the inventory of a *berquil*, with a passing reference to the masonry structures and the wheel (*rouie*) associated with it. At Château de la Cave, the irrigated fruit gardens covered such an extensive amount of acreage in the valley surrounding the palace that a visitor, Count Gabriel Capodolista, was amazed, describing it as an infinite sea of oranges, citrons, and lemons and other 'valuable fruits'.[12] The extent of the gardens is to be expected, since they supplied the king's table, but the key word here is valuable. These fruits were clearly a luxury, even in the eyes of a visiting nobleman.

The subject of luxury brings us to a few words about period eating habits. The French-speaking inhabitants of Cyprus stood out from all the rest of the population because they dressed in the latest style of France. When they entertained at formal banquets and feasts, or when they received guests from Europe, they dined at trestle tables in European fashion, and even served the small *manchet* breads (dinner rolls) that were customary in France during this period. Large roasted joints of meat were delivered to the high table just as they were in Europe, but the sauces and carving were different. Unlike Europeans of this period, the Cypriot nobility ate with two-pronged forks after Byzantine custom, so many dishes were cut up into small pieces, in essence cooked and served like fricassees.

The third or dessert course was more like a mezze in that aside from sweet dishes, small savoury tidbits with accompanying sauces, even fried fish or poached songbirds, could all appear together. The guiding principle was that on meat days meat pervaded the menu all the way to the end. On fish days, fish, sea turtle, and other aquatic animals (including dolphins) filled the menu, with smoked, grilled, or pickled eels taking an inevitable place beside caviar among the sweetmeats and confections.

Eastern dining habits were more or less the rule when the Franks ate informally, for they dined after the Cypriot Greek custom seated on cushions and rugs. Since informal meals were served mezze-fashion (all foods served at once – called in French *service á l'ambigue*), with men eating separately from women, dishes of fruit – raw or cooked – were brought to the table to be sampled according to the mood and discretion of the diner. Because this extraordinary spread of food was to be eaten or simply admired, mezze in this period was strictly an aristocratic meal format, not something found in the houses of commoners, although they may have imitated it according to their means.

Many palaces in Nicosia boasted low stone platforms in a shady part of the courtyard or out under grape arbours so that they could serve as tables when the family chose to eat in a cool place. The dinner hour was generally noon and this was regulated by the church bells in Nicosia's Cathedral of Holy Wisdom as well as by town criers. The bells for matins, dinner, vespers, and other periods of the day were relayed around the island by various Latin monasteries and churches. These bells also regulated the work of the farmers and serfs in the fields. The midday dinner hour was a fixed time in all parts of the island. Shops closed and did not reopen until vespers.

Apple (*Malus spp.*)
Cypriot Frankish: *pommiliers* (apple trees)
Cypriot Greek: *melo* (apple), *mela* (apples), *melia* (apple tree), *melies* (apple trees)

Apples appear twice in the assizes and are spelled each time as *poumes* (plural). It is difficult to know what type of apples were grown on Cyprus, although a study of surviving church paintings and icons might turn up some useful images. They were definitely used in making garlands to ornament rooms and pavilions during feasts and tournaments. There were eight trees at Pefkou, perhaps of more than one variety because sour tasting apples were often used in meat stews. Apples were also converted into confections and dried for use during the winter. Apple pasties and purées like the recipe for apricots given below (p. 18) were common fare during periods of fasting. Meatless days were common on the medieval church calendar; this encouraged the development of many fruit and vegetable-based dishes.

It is evident that some feudal villages devoted part of their energies to fruit production because several have names connected to specific fruits. Katomilla, mentioned in the medieval chronicle of Leontios Makhairas, was a village whose name meant 100 apple trees – the place name is a colloquial corruption of *ekatomelies*.[13] This village gained notoriety because it was the serf Alexis from Katomilla who led a bloody peasant uprising in 1427 and attempted to set himself up as king during the absence of King Janus. He was later captured and executed.

Apricot (*Prunus armeniaca*)
Cypriot Frankish: *hrosomillies* (apricot trees)
Cypriot Greek: *chrysomelo* (apricot), *chrysomela* (apricots); *chrysomelia* (apricot tree), *chrysomelies* (apricot trees)

In Byzantine texts, apricots are called *armeniaka*, and in standard Greek they are called *verikoka*, but in Cyprus they were always known as *chrysomela*, literally 'golden apples.' Apricots are mentioned in the kingdom's assizes in dried form only (pits included), and this is commonly how they were eaten because as a dried fruit they could be stored for quite some time. Otherwise they were preserved in honey or syrup. The actual trees were objects of high value and in the medieval period were largely the property of landowning individuals, especially the landed gentry and nobility. At Pefkou there were three trees, two of which were large (fruit bearing). This would be sufficient to supply the needs of an extended household with fresh fruit while in season, and with dried fruit for the rest of the year.

From a horticultural standpoint, apricots need a great deal of protection from late frosts since they bloom early in the season. The trees at Pefkou may have been planted near a south-facing wall or close to the main house. Nicosia does not experience frosts today, but during the Middle Ages the climate of Cyprus generally was cooler and wetter, so the microclimate may have differed. The 1421 travel account of the Russian monk Zosima described extensive apricot orchards in the area around Kyrenia on the north coast. This part of the island has always enjoyed greater rainfall and is better suited for orchards because it is on the north slope of a mountain range, so that the fruit trees flower late after the threat of frosts has passed.

In cookery, apricots were used in medieval Nicosia in a variety of ways. They were baked in earthenware pots with meat and wine for the Sunday dish known as *psito tis kyriakis*; they were converted into a paste that was served as a confection or used to ornament elaborate dishes; and they were employed extensively in meatless dishes during periods of fasting. One such Cypriot court recipe has been preserved in the medieval German cookbook *Daz Buoch von guoter Spise* (Book of Goodly Fare) compiled about 1350 according to its editor, although I would be tempted to date it closer to 1365–70.[14] There are several other Cypriot recipes in this book; they appear to have been translated into German from a lost Frankish text. In the apricot dish, the Cypriot clue lies in the Frankish name for apricot: *hrosomille*, a word often misconstrued as Jerusalem. The dish in question is a pap or thick soup made from a purée of cooked peaches (substituted for apricots) and almond milk. A translation of the German is provided here:

> *A Mush or Pap*
>
> If one chooses to make a nice pap for Lent, take peaches, mix with thickened almond milk, and cook it well in the milk. Then sprinkle it with sugar. This pap should be called *de hrosomilles*. One eats it cold or hot.

The original German says *von Ierusalem*, but the meaning is clear because of the substitution of peaches for apricots (an ingredient not easily obtainable in medieval Germany). In several published editions of this cookbook, the editors have read *Pirsiche* as 'perch', thus converting it to a strange fish preparation. But *Pfirsiche* is a known dialect word for peach, and this is the type of Lenten fare that upper-class Cypriots ate with a spoon from silver, gold, or Chinese porcelain bowls.[15] In medieval culinary texts, any use of the word 'Jerusalem' should be a red flag pointing to the Cypriot origin of the recipe because it was only in the Frankish of Cyprus that the Cypriot Greek word for apricots was used.

Damask Rose (*Rosa damascena*)
Cypriot Frankish: *tradafillies* (damask rose bushes)
Cypriot Greek: *triantaphyllo* (damask rose), *triantaphylla* (damask roses), *triantaphyllia* (damask rose bush), *triantaphyllies* (damask rose bushes)

The Frankish name is derived directly from the Greek. The root meaning of the Greek name is quite literal: thirty petals in reference to the number found on each flower. Aside from the fact that the inventory provides us with a plural (more than one bush), no specific quantity is given for the number of rose bushes in the garden. Thus it is not possible to determine their precise use. If there were several bushes, there would be enough petals to make rose petal preserves (*triantaphyllo glyko*), which were often used with poultry. The petals can also be dried for use during the winter, and of course they can be used to flavour any number of preparations. However, for the production of rosewater, which was known in Cyprus even in the Byzantine period – and perhaps much earlier, many plants would be required. Glass alembics for distilling rose water have been found in archaeological sites; this suggests that this was a specialized industry.[16] Large amounts of rosewater were used by medieval Cypriots for cosmetics and in their bath houses, where it was added to the hot water and used as a bracer for the skin. It was also a standard ingredient, along with musk and other rarities, in the cookery of the high nobility. But since it was produced at several monasteries, it was also available to people living in the countryside, away from the concentrated wealth of Nicosia and Famagusta.

A Sunday stew, which might serve as the central feature of a *mezze* for a wealthy Greek villager or petty nobleman, could consist of small pieces of goat or pork lungs (or some other type of offal) cooked tender in sesame oil, to which fried meatballs, cinnamon, and cumin would be added. The whole would be thickened with ground chickpeas and mastic, and then sprinkled with rosewater before serving. The juice of sour pomegranates might be added to acidulate the flavours.

Fig (*Ficus carica*)
Cypriot Frankish: *fiers* (fig trees)
Cypriot Greek: *syko* (fig), *syka* (figs), *sykia* (fig tree), *sykies* (fig trees)

There were eight fig trees at Pefkou, but we have no indication of their age or size. If they were large, this number of trees would certainly supply ample fruit for the household. An entire monograph could be written on the role of figs in medieval Cypriot diet; suffice to say they were an important source of nutrition for all economic classes. They were even served fresh or dried in taverns and inns. It was only in the manner in which they were prepared for table that great differences appeared between their urban and rural consumption.

For the well off, *prassa krassata me syka* (leeks stewed with figs and wine in a *ttavas* bake-pot) might serve as the focal dish of a meal during periods of fasting. In the Lefkara area, a recipe for an extremely old fig confection has been preserved in several families; in concept it certainly dates from Byzantine times. Called *sykopittes* (fig patties or fig loaf), it is made by mashing cooked dried figs to a fine paste along with halved almonds and coarsely ground aniseed. This is formed into large balls, which are then pressed down to make patties or cakes. The cakes are then dried. They are eaten sliced as a confection. There are several variations of this basic recipe, with walnuts or the much less expensive pistachios taking the place of almonds.

Dried figs were also put up in a sticky preserve made by cooking them in carob syrup, the *miel noir* of the Franks, or carob honey as it is literally called in Cypriot Greek. And they figure in one of the oldest Greek Cypriot recipes preserved in a medieval manuscript: *dhaktyla,* transmitted via English under the Frankish heading *tourtelettes en friture*.[17] French-speaking Cypriots used the term *tourtelette* for a wide variety of small pastries.

Grapes (*Vitis vinifera*)
Cypriot Frankish: *traillies* (trellised grapes, grapes growing on an arbour)
Cypriot Greek: *klima* (grape vine), *klimata* (grape vines)

The grape vines at Pefkou are described in the inventory as trellised. The French term *traillies* is further clarified by the Cypriot term *klimata*. The meaning of *klimata* in this context is fairly clear: there are numerous grape vines trained to grow on overhead arbours so that the grapes could be harvested from below. This system of viticulture was common in the hot lowland areas of Cyprus even in Roman times because it allowed for a flow of air to pass through the vines and it protected the fruit from extreme heat. It is easy to find images from Byzantine manuscripts showing how this was done. More important, in a city garden like Pefkou, these arbours probably also served as a place where people could sit and eat out of doors. The number of trellises is given in the inventory as four, but this does not convey anything about their size or the number of vines involved. The trellises could have been quite extensive, and they could have been arranged in a quadrant around the cistern. All we can determine is that four separate trellis structures were free standing and not built against one of the houses.

Aside from eating fresh grapes during the course of a meal, the green (unripe) grapes of several Cypriot varietals were used extensively in cookery, especially for making *verjus*. Sour-tasting *verjus*, or *xynostafilo* as it is called in Cypriot Greek, was used like vinegar to temper the taste and medical qualities of medieval recipes. It is not as sharp and cutting as vinegar, and in the hands of the right sort of cook, it could add an elegant touch to many dishes. On the opposite end of the ripening process, grapes picked from the vine and ripened in the hot sun for several days, or grapes fully botrytized on the vines by a fungal condition known as "noble rot", were considered appropriate for desserts and confectionery.

Certainly one of the oldest grape confections still prepared in Cyprus is the sweet, sticky food known in Cypriot Greek as *mahes*. Botrytized grapes are sealed into an earthenware jar and allowed to ferment for several months. The jam-like result, which is also quite alcoholic, is eaten on bread or used as filling in pasties. In former times, *mahes* was much more extensively made, especially as a Christmas confection. It was considered a rare delicacy because the climate of Cyprus does not encourage botrytizing, so the quantity of grapes collected for this preparation was always small.

There is not much doubt about the antiquity of *mahes,* which belonged to a category of thick sticky pastes known as electuaries. The Greek physician Galen mentioned this type of grape confection in his treatise on foodstuffs, so aside from its pleasant flavour, it was also treated as a medicine. In the context of medieval Cyprus, this was probably the only real homemade 'sweet' that most villagers knew. *Pastelli,* a toffee made from carob syrup (*teratsomelo*), and *gruta* (a soft candy made from barley starch and *epsima* – grape must syrup) were also common, but generally sold by vendors who traveled from place to place.

It would be difficult to second guess the inventory regarding the type of grapes grown at Pefkou, but certainly one of the common white varieties grown in Cyprus at this time was the Muscat of Alexandria (also known as *Malaga blanca*). This grape traces its origin to the Cape of Zibibb near Alexandria, and it is the name of this cape that provided medieval Cypriot Greek with the term *zibibi*, strictly speaking, a raisin dried from this varietal. It would appear, however, that even in Arabic *zibib* came to mean any raisin of extra special quality, in particular raisins of unusual size. In his *L'isola de Mondo* (Padua, 1576), Tommaso Porachi described Cypriot *zibibi* as large, black and dried naturally on the vines. These were probably raisins vine-dried from the indigenous

Mavro grape, which the Venetians transplanted to Crete and Cythera for raisin production in the early 1500s. Today Mavro is by far the most widely grown blue grape on the island, and it does well in lowland areas. Even though the fruit is dark blue, its name in Greek means black.

The medieval term *zibibi* (or *zibibe* in Frankish) was certainly in common use in Famagusta and Nicosia, where there were high concentrations of Italian and Spanish merchants, although it may not have been used in the highlands where Greek Cypriot culture was more isolated from outside contacts. Today Cypriots use the standard Greek term for raisin *stafidi* (singular) or *stafidia* (plural). They are known as *stafida* when dried off the stem, and *stafithkia* when allowed to go to raisins on the vines. *Stafithkia* – the true *zibibi* of medieval Cyprus – were used in making sweet raisin wines and sweet wines fermented with other fruits, especially raisin-fig wine.

The Muscat of Alexandria grape was also used to make sweet yellow wines like the once famous Zibibi of Seville mentioned in Arab texts from Spain.[18] In addition, this varietal had a practical culinary application, for its leaves are large and not heavily indented like the leaves of many other grapes. This made them ideal for stuffed grape leaves or *koupepia* as they are called in Cyprus. (Today this role has been filled by the leaves of the sultana grape, a varietal introduced to Cyprus in the 1920s.) The Muscat of Alexandria, like Cypriot Mavro and the ubiquitous white Xynisteri, was a popular lowland grape because it could withstand the intense desert heat of the Cypriot summer. But there were other varietals that also thrived in this climate, some specifically described in period records as Armenian in origin. In total, there are about 16 grape varietals known to be indigenous to Cyprus, plus several others that left the island during the Middle Ages, among them the Altesse de Lucy of Savoy (called Furmint in Hungary), and the famous Savagnin of the French Jura.

Jujube (*Zizyphus jujuba*)
Cypriot Frankish: *zizifies* (jujube bushes)
Cypriot Greek: *zizipho* (jujube berry), *zizipha* (jujube berries), *ziziphia* (jujube tree), *ziziphiés* (jujube trees); modern Cypriot now uses *konnara* (jujube berries) rather than the older Greek form

The jujube probably came to Cyprus with the mulberry during the period of Byzantine agricultural reform in the sixth century AD. This thorny Asian import was one of many innovative ideas borrowed from Sassanian Persia. The plant was initially an exotic in the gardens of the Cypriot nobility and remained so throughout the Byzantine period. As a medical plant, its high value continued into the era of the Lusignans, and the fruits appeared only in the cookery of the nobility – the same could be said for its role in Arab cuisine of this period. Since the Middle Ages, it has naturalized in a few places in lowland areas of Cyprus, but reports of old groves from the eighteenth and nineteenth centuries would seem to suggest that it was considered an orchard crop until recent times.

At Pefkou there were eight trees, enough to produce a huge quantity of fruit. The sticky seedy berries were eaten fresh or dried, and were always considered an important feature of the dessert course among the Franks. There were many types of jujubes in medieval Cyprus, some bronze-red; others pale yellow or almost white, and as sweet as pineapples. Cooks of the period knew how to take them apart and use their honey-like flavours to enhance court dishes of considerable elegance and sophistication. A typical preparation might include lamb or kid, boned and chopped into small pieces, and then stewed with fresh whole jujubes until they are 'plump', then flavouring the dish with musk or *blattes de Bysance*[19] and colouring it yellow with saffron.

Aside from its medical and culinary uses, the thorny branches of the jujube were placed in trees around ripening fruit in order to impale or at least discourage fruit bats, which are a serious nighttime pest in gardens all over the island.

Mulberry (*Morus spp.*)
Cypriot Frankish: *sicaminie* (mulberry trees)
Cypriot Greek: *sykamo* (mulberry), *sykama* (mulberries), *sykamia* (mulberry tree), *sykamies* (mulberry trees); Cypriot Greek also uses *sykomoria* (mulberry tree), and *vavatsino/vavatsina* for the fruit (singular and plural)

The garden inventory states that there were both large (mature) trees and small ones and that the grand total of both came to 30. This would cover a large area of ground and would certainly imply that silk production was one of the purposes of this orchard.

Unfortunately, *sicaminie* includes both *Morus alba* and *Morus nigra*. The white mulberry (*Morus alba*) was grown extensively on the island for the production of silk. With the introduction of the silk industry from Egypt in the

Byzantine Period, Cypriot damask became famous for its high quality and beauty. During the Middle Ages, the silk industry was largely in the hands of the Lusignans, who also owned a royal dye works in Nicosia to process the silk.

In any case, the wood of the white mulberry was commonly used for chair making; the fruits were used medicinally and in cookery. White mulberries were stewed with poultry such as chicken, whereas red mulberries were eaten raw, stewed as compotes, dried or cooked in confections. A wine was also fermented from the red fruit. In the scheme of period dietetics, mulberries were considered astringent and therefore good for the stomach, so they were often taken at the end of meals. In Nicosia, where snow from Mount Olympus (stored in pits lined with straw) was delivered to the royal court year round, it was mixed with mulberry syrup to make a cooling sorbet.

Olive (*Olea europaea*)
Cypriot Frankish: *Olivier, petite* (small olive tree)
Cypriot Greek: *elia* (olive), *elies* (olives), *eleodentro* (olive tree), *eleodentra* (olive trees); Cypriot Greeks also use *elia* and *elies* to designate the tree or trees

In ancient Cyprus the temples owned many of the olive orchards and most of the olive presses, since oil was used in religious rituals. This pattern of ownership was later transferred to the Greek Church, which continued to own most of the olive presses until recent times.[20] The Lusignans closed down a number of Greek monasteries in part to gain control of important olive orchards and turn them over to Latin ownership. Politics and Church power struggles aside, olive trees were not one of the defining features of a valuable fruit garden, which is perhaps why we find only one olive tree at Pefkou. And it is a young tree at that, so its economic value was minimal. Its presence here would make sense if it were a special variety (there were many kinds of olives in medieval Cyprus), perhaps one that was especially plump or succulent.

While olives were associated with everyday foods like *elies taskistes me koliandros* (cracked green olives with coriander), they were especially important during times of fasting. Olive bread (*elioti*) was eaten during this time, and olives, but not olive oil, were also allowed. Most medieval Cypriots cooked with sesame oil and filled lamps with coarse grades of olive oil. High-grade olive oil, of the sort now promoted by food enthusiasts, was as much a luxury in the Middle Ages as it is today.

Orange (*Citrus aurantium* and *Citrus sinensis*)
Cypriot Frankish: *neragies* or *nerangies*
Cypriot Greek: *neratzo* (orange), *neratza* (oranges), *neratzia* (orange tree), *neratziés* (orange trees). Also written *nerantzo*, *portokalia*, etc., depending on one's spoken dialect

At Pefkou there were seven orange trees, one free standing and six espaliered against the wall of a house (*après de l'ostel*). Oranges are generally planted in a protected location in Cyprus to reduce wind damage and exposure to untimely frosts. Nearly every medieval reference we have to orange trees places them within cloisters or courtyard gardens. The espaliered oranges at Pefkou were probably planted along a south-facing wall. When planted in an open field they are always surrounded by a windbreak of cypress trees. This was doubtless the intended function of the hedge that surrounded the garden of Pefkou.

Oranges were a daily feature of the court cuisine of Cyprus and they appeared in several ways. The sour orange (*Citrus aurantium*) was definitely on the island by AD 1000 and perhaps earlier (the Byzantines called it *nerántzion*). It provided acidulation in cookery much as lemon juice does today. It is called *kitromilo* in modern Cypriot and resembles a mandarin orange in shape and size. Historically, it was boiled with sugar to make confections, especially a type of paste that could be sliced and eaten like candy. The juice was also used like vinegar in *zaladina* (pork aspic). Pictures of oranges from this period show *kitromila* placed on the water carafes that were used at table for mixing wine with water, acting as a stopper to keep out flies. I suspect that when finger bowls were passed, these same oranges were squeezed into the water because the acid would help take grease off the hands.

Sweet oranges, called *portokalia* in medieval Cypriot Greek, were first reported in 1433 at the monastery of des Prêtres (*tou Ieréon*) where a monk noted in the marginalia of a book that the trees had been damaged in a windstorm.[21] This is one of the earliest references to sweet oranges in the Mediterranean and throws open to question the whole manner in which they were supposedly introduced from Goa in 1498.

Lastly, the rinds of oranges had a non-culinary use. Oranges were peeled to keep the bottom half of the rind intact. This served as a cup that was set into a bowl or lamp and filled with oil. A wick was lit and as the oil burned down, the room was filled with the scent of orange – a medieval version of aromatherapy.

Peach (*Prunus persica*)
Cypriot Frankish: *rodaquinies* (peach trees)
Cypriot Greek: *rodakino* (peach), *rodakina* (peaches); *rodakinia* (peach tree), *rodakiniés* (peach trees)

While peaches are said to have been cultivated in the Mediterranean region for several thousand years, they are not mentioned in the assizes, and there is a real question about the date of their introduction into Cyprus. They do not appear very often in medieval Arab cookbooks either. Precise data for the period prior to the Lusignans is lacking, and archaeological evidence in the form of peach pits from the Middle Ages is not at all complete enough to draw broad conclusions.

Written evidence suggests that peaches were not common, and yet at Pefkou we find 20 trees. Dried peaches were probably one of the mainstays of the Sis household during the winter, and as such a valid substitute in the purée recipe discussed under apricots (p. 18). The large number of trees might also reflect an ethnic food preference on the part of Armenian Cypriots, or it may be quite pragmatic: peaches are highly productive and require less nurturing than apricots and plums. However, I am inclined to think that the peach, in this period at least, was a status food. Ripe peaches, like dates, were considered appropriate for the first course, which generally centred on some type of gruel. Peaches marinated in wine (to remove their astringency) were normally served after roasts of meat. It was up to the court physician to determine what combinations of foods were best suited to the king and his consort.

Pine (*Pinus spp.*)
Cypriot Frankish: *pin*
Cypriot Greek: *pefkos*

Although it is difficult to draw out hidden meanings from garden documents due to the fluid nature of plant taxonomy, certain truisms can be established regarding the 'great tree' in the garden at Pefkou. We can eliminate *Pinus niger* (*mantopefkos*) which towers over all other pine trees in Cyprus but can only be found in the wild in the rugged terrain of the Troodos Mountains in areas higher than 1200 metres above sea level.

Next in line is *Pinus brutia* which is the common native pine tree of the Cypriot lowlands. *Pinus brutia* is best considered a lumber pine; it grows very tall where it is left to reach maturity (24 to 40 metres). It was used extensively in house construction (rafters for example), especially in the mud-brick buildings that once characterized the lowland architecture of Cyprus. It was also used in the half-timber buildings erected by the Franks. This is not a graceful tree but it withstands the intense summer heat on the island and its filtered shade creates ecological niches for many types of useful wild plants.

If we presume that all the plants at Pefkou were cultivated varieties as opposed to wild ones, as the inventory seems to confirm, then the only logical candidate for the Pefkou pine would be the stone pine (*Pinus pinea*). Because of its economic importance, the stone pine makes the most sense since it is the only pine identified in medieval and renaissance herbals as a true domesticate. It was called *Pinus sativus urbana* in medieval medical treatises, in reference to its popularity as a garden plant. The stone pine provides aromatic shade, certain medical benefits from its needles, and yields pine nuts which have high commercial value. It is not native to Cyprus, but it was planted in private gardens even in Byzantine times, so some botanists consider it indigenous. A royal garden with a massive stone pine at its centre would not have been unusual. Pefkou is probably a good representation of the type of garden employed by the lower levels of Frankish aristocracy to support the lifestyle that was equated by Europeans with high life in the East. In any event, pine nuts were a critical ingredient in the diet of this luxurious way of living because they were important to the success of sauces, dips, stews and so many other dishes representative of court cuisine. Since pine nuts were only found in private gardens like Pefkou, it is probably safe to assume that out in the villages this was not an ingredient in local cookery during the Middle Ages.

The pine cones on the de Pin coat-of-arms may be those of the stone pine. This type of metaphorical play on symbolism buried in the artifacts of the Lusignan kingdom provides an interesting avenue for deconstructing the values and mind-set of the major players involved. The de Pin family, like so many of the others who came to the *Outremere*, may have expropriated a local symbol for their coat-of-arms. They would not have been the first to do this. In this light, there is another possible explanation for the name of Pefkou: it may derive from the family name de Pin or de Pins.

The de Pins were powerful members of the upper nobility of Cyprus. Odo de Pin was Grand Master of the Order of St John of Jerusalem from 1294 to 1295, and from 1355 to 1365 Roger de Pin served in the same office. Roger was an important ally of King Peter I and accompanied him when he captured

Alexandria. The family's private chapel and crypt was located in the gothic Cathedral of Holy Wisdom (now a mosque) in the Turkish occupied section of Nicosia. A private chapel in the cathedral was an honour enjoyed only by a select few in medieval Cyprus, and the family coat-of-arms is still displayed there as well as on one of the exterior walls of the cathedral. It consists of a red shield with three golden pine cones. Was this property called du Pin because members of this family once occupied it and planted the pine tree there as a symbol of their presence? All we know for certain is that by 1468 the Cypriot de Pins were extinct, the land belonged to the Crown, and that the pine tree growing there was some sort of a local landmark.

In view of this, it is striking that adjacent to the garden we not only have a monastic community connected with Kellaki (a holding of the Order of St John of Jerusalem), but a church of Saint Evstathios. The Byzantine church of Ayios Evstathios at Kolossi Castle was used by the Order of St John as its private chapel. This is not coincidental: Saint Eustace was a martyred Roman general whose adoptive name meant good fortune; thus he offered important psychological values to the 'soldiers' belonging to the Order of St John. More importantly, Eustace was the saint of the hunt. Every nobleman in Cyprus, member of the Order of St John or otherwise, went to the priests of St Eustace to have their hounds and falcons blessed before they went off into the woods for sport. To have this church so close to a royal property as well as to a property connected with the Order of St John suggests that this was probably a chapel of convenience for all the aristocratic huntsmen in the neighbourhood. And if the hunters were successful, we can assume that Papa Prokopis and his wife enjoyed some excellent game dinners.

Plum (*Prunus* spp.)
Cypriot Frankish: *bournelies* (plum trees)
Cypriot Greek: *bournela* (plum), *bourneles* (plums); *bournelia* (plum tree), *bourneliés* (plum trees)

The plum is such a diverse group, with so many sub-species and hybrids, that it is difficult to know for certain what exactly was being grown at Pefkou. The inventory makes it clear that there were two different types of tree (one of each): *bourneliés*, and an ordinary or common one. This would seem to imply one plum for a special use such as eating out of hand and one for drying. The special one was not known to the Franks, hence the need to borrow the name from Greek. While this is still hazy in terms of variety, it is clearly not a prune plum, which would be *damaskino* in Cypriot Greek. In modern standard Greek, *damaskino* applies to Mirabelle plums.

It is known from eighteenth-century accounts that there were two plums considered distinctive to Cyprus. One had large blue fruit while the other was the same colour but much smaller. Both were similar in appearance to European damsons. But there were also scattered reports of yellow plums and plums not quite typical of what was found in Europe. Perhaps the true *bournela* was something akin to the modern greengage (*Prunus domestica institia*) because it was native to the region yet unknown at this time in Europe. It is interesting that the numbers of plum trees and apricots are roughly equal, while the number of peach trees (20 in all) far exceeds the needs of a large household. In terms of consumption, this tends to place apricots and plums far behind peaches in economic importance, at least at Pefkou.

Pomegranate
Cypriot Frankish: *pommesgranades*
Cypriot Greek: *rodhi* (pomegranate), *rodhia* (pomegranates), *rodhia* (pomegranate tree or bush), *rodhies* (pomegranate trees or bushes)

The most important plants in the royal garden of Pefkou were the pomegranates. There were 120 shrubs, which would cover considerable ground unless they were pruned into hedges, which is possible. The editors of *Le livre des remembrances* presumed that these plants were purely ornamental. I do not share that opinion. Nothing else in the garden was ornamental and just because the inventory lists the pomegranates as *sans fruit* this is not to say that they were barren. The inventory was taken on June 16, 1468 and at that time of the year most of the other plants are at least beginning to set fruit. Pomegranates are only starting to flower, so there would be no ripe fruit on them until about November. From the sheer number of plants, it is obvious that the pomegranate played a crucial role in the diet of medieval Cypriots. This is not surprising. This plant has been cultivated on the island since ancient times, and was intimately connected with the cult of Aphrodite. The goddess is said to have been the first to plant it on Cyprus, a claim often repeated, even in medieval texts.

Cypriot pomegranates were classified as sweet or sour, but both types were essentially the same colour: white fleshed ranging to pale pink. There was also a seedless variety called *kouforova*. The red pomegranates popular today were not introduced until very recent times. Sweet pomegranates provided fruit for eating out of hand; the arils (the jellylike mass containing the seeds) were scattered over food or mixed into cooked dishes. The typical *sauce Sarasine* of the Lusignan court was understood to mean a sauce coloured red with Syrian rue (*Peganum harmala*) and garnished with pomegranate arils. The arils were even dried and ground to a powder for flavouring various preparations. The sour pomegranates served the role of lemons in ancient and medieval Cyprus and were universally consumed. The juice was cooked to make sweet syrup called *grenade* or to make sour *verjus* that could be stored in jars or bottles. But sour pomegranates stored well, so they could be kept most of the year and crushed for juice as required.

In Cyprus, there is a dietary need for this sour element in food because the water on the island is extremely hard, thus gravel and kidney stones are widespread. Today, Cypriots put lemon juice on just about everything partly for this reason. In the Middle Ages, they used pomegranate juice, a food habit shared with the mainland, especially Syria and the region now known as Lebanon. Lemons, which are much easier to squeeze and not quite as sour, were a luxury fruit in medieval Cyprus and gave a distinctive taste to the cuisine of the well-to-do. Two types of lemons known in this period were the Georgian lemon, introduced via Constantinople, and the Palestine sweet lemon (*Citrus limettoides*), which originated in India.

Sorb Apple (*Sorbus domestica*)?
Cypriot Frankish: Pommelier de Saint Johan (apples of St John)
Cypriot Greek: none given

The identity of the two trees called 'apples of St John' is not a settled matter. The editors of *Le livre des remembrances* suggested that since this term is used in the French Midi for the *Amelanchier ovalis* (European Juneberry), this is probably what was intended. I disagree. The Juneberry is a wild fruit not found in Cyprus, and all of the plants at Pefkou are clearly domesticated. Furthermore, the Juneberry is not a high-value fruit; it was foraged food for country people even in the Midi. A plant vaguely similar to the Juneberry, but native or naturalized since ancient times, was the sebesten tree or Assyrian plum (*Cordia myxa*), which was cultivated for its drupes, especially for their medical uses. On the other hand, this was well known to Cypriots under the name *myxia*, a source of a sticky substance employed in snaring birds.

Plants bearing the name of St John the Baptist were thought to have miraculous and healing powers. They generally came to flower or fruit around the time of St John's Day (June 24), a feast given the status of a Solemnity (feast of the highest order) by the Latin Church. This was also one of the most important feast days for the Order of St John of Jerusalem, which celebrated it in Cyprus with great processions and jousts. June 24 was the saint's official birthday, but his death on August 29 was also observed by the Order.

The mysterious fruit trees mentioned in the contract must derive their name from a connection either with June 24 or August 19. But since this term has not been found anywhere else in Frankish documents, and since there is no Greek equivalent given, we must suppose this to be a plant not well-known to Cypriot Greeks, but which had a local Frankish name. This means it must have been an exotic cultivated only in the gardens of the nobility. We could read the entry quite literally: apple trees belonging to the Order of St John (a legal possibility). But I think one logical alternative would be the sorb apple (*Sorbus domestica*) because it flowers during midsummer in northern Europe and is in full fruit in Cyprus about the same time.

The sorb apple was popular in French medieval gardens but was always extremely rare in Cyprus, although more common in neighbouring Asia Minor. Meikle recorded only two known trees from a nineteenth-century survey, but noted that they were probably relics from an earlier time when the plant was cultivated on the island. The fact that the sorb apple was only known as a garden plant would further strengthen the case here. Furthermore there were apple- and pear-shaped varieties, and while the fruit is mealy, its high sugar content makes it ideal for confectionery, liquors, and for processing wine. It was also used extensively in medieval medicine.

However, since we know very little about the cookery of the Armenian Kingdom of Cilicia, and the dietary preferences of the émigrés to Cyprus, this one corner of the garden at Pefkou must remain for the time an unknown.

Walnut (*Juglans spp.*)
Cypriot Frankish: *nolier* (walnut tree), *noliers* (walnut trees)
Cypriot Greek: *karidi* (walnut), *karidia* (walnuts), *karidia* (walnut tree), *karidies* (walnut trees)

The importance of the walnut in medieval Cypriot diet cannot be overemphasized, although it is clear that it was consumed mostly on festive occasions, aside from its perceived medical properties. Walnuts were generally grown in the hill country where it was cooler. The Petite Commanderie of La Fenique and La Noyére, one of the manorial properties of the Order of St John of Jerusalem in the medieval bailiwick of Evdimou, produced large quantities of walnuts for sale and for the use of the order. La Noyére means 'the walnut grove', a place name that survives as the modern village of Anoyira.

The English walnut (*Juglans regia*) is the most common species of walnut on the island. While not native, it was introduced into Cyprus in ancient times and has even naturalized in some places. It is an extremely high-value tree but must be cultivated in localities where there is sufficient rainfall or a source of water (La Noyére has a stream running through it). From the garden inventory for Pefkou, which lists three trees, it is clear that one mature walnut tree was growing by the cistern; the two small trees could not have been too far away. The nuts of the walnut were used extensively in the medieval cookery of both the Franks and native Greeks. The preserve made of small green walnuts and syrup known as *glyko karidaki* is one of the oldest types of dessert foods made in Cyprus. Prior to the introduction of sugar, it was made with honey or date sugar, or even carob syrup.

In some parts of Cyprus, it was a custom to plant a walnut tree at the birth of a female child so that by the time she was married, the tree would supply wood for her dowry furniture, especially the chest in which she stored her wedding goods. This custom, which survived into recent times, may have evolved as an imitation of a practice among feudal landowners because as a rule walnut trees in medieval Cyprus did not belong to peasant farmers. The presence of two baby walnut trees at Pefkou might be interpreted as circumstantial evidence that the custom dates from the medieval period; if they had been specifically mentioned in the contract as dower trees we would have positive proof.

Wild Fruits not Brought under Cultivation

Outside the precincts of the irrigated gardens of the well-to-do, there were many wild fruits that played an important role in medieval Cypriot diet. Some, like the Mediterranean medlar and the turpentine tree, were actually planted on marginal ground so that they would be readily available when needed. A number of these fruits were harvested for wreaths and garlands for Advent, Christmas and Twelfth Night (Christmas for the Greek Church). The coat-of-arms of Queen Charlotte de Lusignan, which appears on a bookplate in a volume she gave to the Pope as a gift, shows her arms surrounded by one of the popular Lusignan wreaths used at court: leaves of oleander ornamented with the fruits of the Mediterranean medlar and the strawberry tree. Charlotte was doubtless aware of the Cypriot symbolism in these native plants and the intermingling of mythologies about Aphrodite with her own genealogical claims of an ancestress called Melusine who was half woman and half fish.

Important Wild Fruits with their Cypriot Names

Bramble (*Rubus sanctus*)
Cypriot Greek: *vatos, vramos*
Common Hawthorn (*Crataegus monogyna Jacq.*)
Cypriot Greek: *kokkinomosphilia*
Cornelian Cherry (*Cornus mas*)
Cypriot Greek: *kerazia, krania*
Dog Rose (*Rosa canina L.*)
Cypriot Greek: *agriotriantaphylia, moushietta*
Mastic Tree (*Pistacia lentiscus L*)
Cypriot Greek: *shinia, skinos*
Medlar (*Mespilus germanica*)
Cypriot Greek: *pomelithkia*
Mediterranean Medlar (*Crataegus azarolus L.*)
Cypriot Greek: *mosphylia*
Strawberry Tree (*Arbutus andrachne* and *Arbutus unedo*).
Cypriot Greek: *andruklia*
Sumac (*Rhus coriaria*)
Cypriot Greek: *soumaki, roudi*
Turpentine Tree (*Pistacia terebinthus L.*)
Cypriot Greek: *trimithia*

Footnotes

1. Claude D. Cobham, *Excerpta Cypria: Materials for a History of Cyprus* (Cambridge, 1908), p. 35. I have corrected Cobham's translation of the Italian in several places since he had trouble with plant and gardening terms. The squills mentioned in the quote are also called sea onions (*Urginea maritima*). They were an export crop raised for their high medical value. The Cornaros received Episkopi as a titular fief in 1398 and held the property until it was expropriated by the Turks in 1570.

    Regarding the bananas, the Frankish word for banana was *musse*, from Sanskrit *musa*. They also called the plant the Apple of Paradise (*pomme de Paradis*), one of its names in Arabic, and as such considered it a relic of the Bible. The bananas of medieval Cyprus were the Eumusa type, with pendant rather than erect fruit. Bananas were introduced into Cyprus as soon as they were known in Alexandria and were well established by AD 1000, especially in the Paphos area, where they can be grown in the open due to the hot, humid microclimate. In other lowland areas, they were planted in courtyards or walled gardens to protect them from cutting winter winds.

2. An excellent medieval insight into the 'tempering' of foods based on Galenic medicine and dietetics can be found in Terrence Scully's 'The Opusculum de Saporibus of Magninus Mediolanensis,' *Medium Aevum*, 54:2 (1985), 178–207. For Galen's own words on the subject, refer to Mark Grant, *Galen on Food and Diet* (London: Routledge, 2000).

3. Jean Richard and Theodore Papadopoullos, 'Le livre des remembrances de la secrète du royaume de Chypre (1468–1469)', in *Sources et études de l'histoire de Chypre*, X (Nicosia: Cyprus Research Centre, 1983). The entire volume is devoted to this text.

4. R. M. Dawkins, *The Chronicle of George Boustronios 1456–1489* (Melbourne: Melbourne University Press, 1964).

5. W. H. Rudt de Collenberg, 'Les Luisignan de Chypre', in Επετηρις, X (Nicosia, 1979–80), 196.

6. For example, in 1233 King Henry I sold the presterie of Timios Stavros to the Archbishop of Nicosia; this land was within the city walls and adjacent to another property also described as a presterie. See Nicholas Coureas and Christopher Schabel, eds., *The Cartularly of the Cathedral of Holy Wisdom of Nicosia* (Nicosia, 1997), 154–5.

7   Refer to Ioannis Ionas, *Pottery in the Cyprus Tradition* (Nicosia, 1998), 37. The author describes the *ttavas* but does not provide details on its origins. For more information, see Edna Stern, 'Ceramic Ware from the Crusader Period in the Holy Land', in Sylvia Rozenberg, ed., *Knights of the Holy Land* (Jerusalem, 1999), 259–265.
8   For details on the history of the Kingdom of Cilicia, refer to Angus Donal Stewart, *The Armenian Kingdom and the Mamluks* (Leiden: Brill, 2001).
9   George Hill, *A History of Cyprus* (Cambridge, 1948), vol. 3, 22.
10 Susanna Lyle, *Fruit & Nuts: A Comprehensive Guide* (Portland: The Timber Press, 2006).
11 I refer here to the ancient laws of the burgess courts. See Nicholas Coureas, ed. and trans., *The Assizes of the Lusignan Kingdom of Cyprus* (Nicosia, 2002). Coureas translated the Greek versions of the assizes. The original laws were written in French.
12 Leontis Makhairas, *Recital Concerning the Sweet Land of Cyprus*, R. M. Dawkins, ed. (Oxford, 1932), vol. 2, 199 notes. Facsimile reprint by Editions L'Oiseau, Famagusta, Cyprus, n.d. (c. 1966–74).
13 Makhairas, vol. 1, 677
14 I refer the reader to the most up-to-date edition of this text edited by Melitta Weiss Adamson, *Daz Buoch von guoter Spise* (Krems, 2004). This was published as an off-print of volume IX of *Medium Aevum Quotidianum*. The recipe in question appears on page 82.
15 Famagusta was the main conduit to the West for the China trade via overland Asian routes. To date, no archaeological work has been done on this at Famagusta, although the site is ripe for exploration. For the Alexandria connection in this trade network, see Véronique François, *Ceramiques médiévals à Alexandrie* (Paris: Institute Française d'Archéologique Oriental, 1999).
16 The rebirth of the Cypriot damask rose industry at Agros during the 1920s is covered in a monograph by Ioannis Katzepetras. *Η Τριανταφυλλια και τα Προιντα της* (Nicosia, 1992). The Agros firm of Chris N. Tsolakis is now the largest producer on the island.
17 This recipe is preserved in the English cookery book called *Form of Cury* dating from the 1390s. For the original text, refer to Constance Hieatt and Sharon Butler, eds., *Curye on Inglysch* (Oxford, 1985), 132. I will paraphrase the recipe: 'Take figs and grind them small, then add saffron and spice powder. Wrap this in "foyles" of dough (read *phyllo* here) and fry them

in oil. Clarify honey and pour this over them. Serve hot or cold.' While the recipe is corrupt, this is the essential outline for *dakhtyla*, long finger-shaped pastries that take their name from Greek *dakhtylos*. The ends are pressed together with a fork. This recipe is much older than the 1390s collection in which it appears, and its title in the *Form of Cury, tourtelettes en friture*, is not recipe specific. It is the equivalent of a chapter heading for a broad category of small fried pastries, evidence in itself that the recipe was lifted from an older Frankish text that had other pastries in it.

18 For a scientific and oenological analysis of the Muscat of Alexandria, refer to Pierre Galet, *Cépages et vignobles de France* (Montpellier: Paysan du Midi, 1964), vol. 4, 3141–3.

19 *Blattes de Bysance* are the fragrant *opercula* (lids) of wing snails (*Strombus lengtiginosus*). They are about a human thumbnail in size. When cooked, the lids reduce to a musky demi-glace used in medieval Cypriot cuisine. This ingredient had been imported from the Persian Gulf since the Byzantine period and perhaps even earlier.

20 A full account of the role of olives in Cypriot agriculture is given by Sophocles Hadjisavvas in *Olive Oil Processing in Cyprus* (Nicosia: Paul Aströms Förlag, 1992).

21 The annotation is dated October 21, 1433. It was recorded in a marginal diary kept in a Cypriot Greek manuscript dating from 1112. The book is now in Paris. For published information, refer to J. Darrouzès, 'Un obituaire chypriote: Le Parsininus graecus 1588', Κυπριαχαι Σπονδαι 15 (1951), 25–62.

Translation of the 1468 Agreement of Transfer

The document is dated on a Saturday because this was a market day. It was during market, when large numbers of people converged on Nicosia that the burgess courts were held and legal matters transacted. The burgess court, which handled affairs relating to free citizens (as opposed to serfs), was overseen by the viscount of Nicosia, in this case Jayme Zaplana. The records of the burgess court are no longer extant, but we have this copy which was entered into the ledger of the royal treasury outlining what took place. While the nobility had their own courts for transacting legal matters, it would appear that since Theodore, son of Saïd the Syrian, was a commoner, the whole case ended up before Zaplana rather than someone else.

It was Zaplana who appointed the committee of jurats (free citizens serving as assessors) to make a list of what was on the property for tax and rental purposes. This list was given to the new occupant so that he and the royal treasury would have a point of reference should there be a dispute about his upkeep or a need for him to show what improvements he made after June 16, 1468. The list was intended to protect both the Crown and the tenant.

Since the original French was rather awkwardly worded, the translator has taken liberties to transform it into a smooth paraphrase. I also made some small adjustments myself. Ed.

Here follows the proceedings involving the restitution by George of Sis of the lease and quit-rents for the garden of Pefkou, which had belonged to Lady Marie de Fougère, and the subsequent bestowing of this said garden lease and its quit-rents upon Theodore, son of Saïd the Syrian.

On Saturday the sixteenth day of June in the year of Our Lord 1468, before his grace Viscount Jayme Zaplana, Sir Philip Ciba bailiff of the Royal Treasury and Sir Simon Stanbailli, the advisors, and me Andrea Bibi, Sir Thomas Petropoulo, Sir Peter Goul, the royal secretaries, came the said George of Sis, who was responsible for the quit-rents of the garden called Pefkou, which had belonged to Marie de Fougière, bounded on one side by Saint Nicholas of Quellac and on the other by the church of Ayios Evstathios, with all its rights, uses and dependences etc. ... thus all as the aforementioned George holds and uses, came and restored it to the Royal Treasury, the said treasury takes control of this restitution, clears the title of the garden and acquits George of Sis from further financial responsibility concerning the lease and its quit-rents.

On this day, in the presence of the aforementioned, the treasury gives from this time on its rents and title to the rents of the garden which is called Pefkou, which had been Lady Marie of Fougière's, bordering on one side Saint Nicholas of Quellac and on the other side the church of Ayios Evstathios, with all the rights, uses and dependences including buildings, irrigation works, a water wheel, a cistern and all the other things that belonged to the said garden and ought to belong to it, and thus all as the said treasury has and uses or could have and use, to Theodore, son of Saïd the Syrian of Laxia, and to all his heirs by lawful marriage, in payment of 40 besants annually; a quarter (10 besants), must be paid every three months, by the aforementioned Theodore, and all those who will possess the said garden are required and obliged to maintain it in good condition and always improve or repair it and not to abandon it, and if there is failure to comply with any of these conditions, the said treasury has the power to assume repossession of the said garden without dispute or opposition. Item, the said Theodore must receive the said garden by official agreement and in the event that he will want to return it or for any reason would want to vacate it, he is also required to return it by official agreement and this must be prepared according to the practice of the Royal Treasury. And by the aforementioned means and conditions the said treasury has placed Pefkou in possession of the said Theodore son of Saïd and his heirs.

The inventory was made concerning the said garden by the head gardener and the committee of citizens, and father Savas Prokopis, who wrote it down. This list was made on 16 June AD 1468 and was entrusted to Theodore son of Saïd.

A)
Apple Trees VIII
Apricot Trees III
   large II
   small I
Damask Roses
Fig Trees VIII
Grape vines trellised, that is arboured IIII
Jujubes VIII
Mulberry trees, large and small XXX
Olive tree, small I

Orange trees VII
    standing alone I
    against the house VI
Peach trees XX
Pine tree, large I
Plum trees, ordinary II
Pomegranates, without fruit CXX
Apple of St Johan II
Walnut trees, small II
Item: large walnut tree by the cistern I

B)
Unirrigated land
Two parcels of irrigated land
Petra vlacotis dexaminis [reservoir and irrigation ditch in stone. *Ed.*]
The hedge of the garden, one side destroyed
The cistern and its irrigation works
5 *drahti* [term obscure] and a *trief* [term obscure] and a *cleuvi* [term obscure] and an old water wheel without value. [The terms here are technical and cannot be deciphered without an Arab or Greek gloss. It appears that we are dealing with discarded or damaged equipment associated with an elaborate irrigation system. *Ed.*]

C)
Houses
The gate of the garden with a pair of doors. [Some type of stone archway. *Ed.*]
Three houses with three pairs of entrance gates and 18 rafters [each] and two with pillars with plinths, and one without a plinth. [The implication here is that two houses had fine Renaissance style entrances, while the other house was either of a lesser sort, or its entrance gate was in some way damaged. It was common practice in Cyprus to reuse columns retrieved from Greek and Roman ruins since there is no marble found on the island. *Ed.*]